IN FOCUS: ANTI-SEMITISM

Annamária Pongor

IN FOCUS: ANTI-SEMITISM

Anti-Semitism Presented in Arthur Miller's Focus

VDM Verlag Dr. Müller

Impressum/Imprint (nur für Deutschland/ only for Germany)
Bibliografische Information der Deutschen Nationalbibliothek: Die Deutsche Nationalbibliothek verzeichnet diese Publikation in der Deutschen Nationalbibliografie; detaillierte bibliografische Daten sind im Internet über http://dnb.d-nb.de abrufbar.
Alle in diesem Buch genannten Marken und Produktnamen unterliegen warenzeichen-, markenoder patentrechtlichem Schutz bzw. sind Warenzeichen oder eingetragene Warenzeichen der jeweiligen Inhaber. Die Wiedergabe von Marken, Produktnamen, Gebrauchsnamen, Handelsnamen, Warenbezeichnungen u.s.w. in diesem Werk berechtigt auch ohne besondere Kennzeichnung nicht zu der Annahme, dass solche Namen im Sinne der Warenzeichen- und Markenschutzgesetzgebung als frei zu betrachten wären und daher von jedermann benutzt werden dürften.

Coverbild: www.purestockx.com

Verlag: VDM Verlag Dr. Müller Aktiengesellschaft & Co. KG
Dudweiler Landstr. 99, 66123 Saarbrücken, Deutschland
Telefon +49 681 9100-698, Telefax +49 681 9100-988, Email: info@vdm-verlag.de

Herstellung in Deutschland:
Schaltungsdienst Lange o.H.G., Berlin
Books on Demand GmbH, Norderstedt
Reha GmbH, Saarbrücken
Amazon Distribution GmbH, Leipzig
ISBN: 978-3-639-07937-1

Imprint (only for USA, GB)
Bibliographic information published by the Deutsche Nationalbibliothek: The Deutsche Nationalbibliothek lists this publication in the Deutsche Nationalbibliografie; detailed bibliographic data are available in the Internet at http://dnb.d-nb.de.
Any brand names and product names mentioned in this book are subject to trademark, brand or patent protection and are trademarks or registered trademarks of their respective holders. The use of brand names, product names, common names, trade names, product descriptions etc. even without a particular marking in this works is in no way to be construed to mean that such names may be regarded as unrestricted in respect of trademark and brand protection legislation and could thus be used by anyone.

Cover image: www.purestockx.com

Publisher:
VDM Verlag Dr. Müller Aktiengesellschaft & Co. KG
Dudweiler Landstr. 99, 66123 Saarbrücken, Germany
Phone +49 681 9100-698, Fax +49 681 9100-988, Email: info@vdm-verlag.de

Copyright © 2008 by the author and VDM Verlag Dr. Müller Aktiengesellschaft & Co. KG and licensors
All rights reserved. Saarbrücken 2008

Printed in the U.S.A.
Printed in the U.K. by (see last page)
ISBN: 978-3-639-07937-1

1. Introduction

The central theme of the thesis is anti-Semitism as it was and it still is the cause of suffering for many people. The chosen work for the presentation of anti-Semitism is Arthur Miller's *Focus*, one of the greatest novels in American literature.

Miller's novel, *Focus* gives the reader a large number of examples concerning anti-Semitism in the United States, that is considered the most liberal, equal and democratic country in the world. The thesis presents Miller's ability to make Jewish wartime experience become more visible.

The thesis also presets that Anti-Semitism in the United States became obvious at the end of the 1930s, when Europe suffered from the spreading of Nazism and Fascism, and Jewish people were desperately looking for a place where they could feel secure. American public was strongly influenced by voices that suggested that Jews are a threat to the country; they are the enemy of the United States. Jewish inhabitants found themselves in a situation where they had no equal rights with gentiles, they were excluded from social circles, universities, and they could not find a place to work.

Miller's novel shows the reader an unexpected angle, as its central character is not a hero; in fact, he is an anti-Semite, who becomes a protagonist by major changes in his personality.

The thesis presents the moral improvement of Lawrence Newman, who becomes able to see life clearer, without preconceptions when he is considered Jewish. He realises that no one cares about who he is in reality; everybody is concerned with what he appears to be.

Since the time he has to wear glasses, his life is completely turned upside down. Miller's novel shows, that when major catastrophes happen in the world, the same is happening in the souls of innocent people.

The thesis presents Miller's *Focus* as a novel about the growing racial and anti-Semitic tension in the United States, and in the same time as a novel that points out the irrational hatred directed towards any racial minority.

The conclusion of the novel remains, that changes have to occur first in the minds of people, and then laws of the county has to be more severe when there are innocent people who are suffering from others' preconceptions, meanness or stupidity.

The analysis of the novel is based on Christopher Bigsby's *The Cambridge Companion to Arthur Miller,* with special attention on the chapter written by Malcom Bradbury: *Arthur Miller's fiction*; Robert W. Corrigan's *Arthur Miller A Collection of Critical Essays*; and *Arthur Miller,* written by Leonard Moss.

2. Anti-Semitism

Elie Wiesel enlists some contradictions in the foreword Abraham H. Foxman's book, *Never again? The Threat of New Anti-Semitism*:

> "For some, Jews were or are too wealthy; for others, they are or were too poor. Too religious or not enough. Too Jewish or too assimilated. Too learned or too ignorant. Too smart or too naïve. Too nationalistic or too universalist.(…) Hitler believed that all Jews were communists; Stalin was convinced that all Jews were capitalists. Hitler and Stalin were mortal enemies; yet they were united in their hatred of Jews. Thus, anti-Semitism has a wide range of components: religious and social, ethnic and professional, racist and political. No wonder that a French thinker called it "the socialism of the imbeciles" (Foxman, A. H. 2003: IX)

Anti-Semitism is defined as hostile attitudes and actions against Jews. These are based on the belief that Jews are part of a strongly separated nation that is inferior and evil from their birth.

2.1. The Word and its Origin

The word 'anti-Semitic' was first used in1860 by Moritz Steinschneider, a Jewish scholar. He wrote about Ernest Ronan's ideas, and he used the phase 'anti-Semitic prejudices'. Steinschneider used this phrase to analyse Renan's ideas about how 'Semitic races' were inferior to 'Arean Races'. Wilhelm Marr invented the term 'antisemitismus' in his work entitled *The Way to Victory of Germanicism over Judaism*. His main idea was that Jews wanted to dominate the German economy and wanted to degrade Germany. He thought that Jews are mean and they cannot change, because evil is in their blood, and that they are inferior of humankind:

> "Even the most honourable Jews are under the inescapable influence of his blood, career of a Semitic morality totally opposed to Germanic values... aimed at the destruction and burial of German values and tradition..." (Robertson, R. 1999:190)

Semitic means a member of a people speaking a Semitic language, in particular the Jews and Arabs. Anti-Semitism means hostility or prejudice against Jews.

The word is made of the Greek words 'anti' meaning against and 'Semite', meaning descendent of Shem. Shem was the second son of Noah who became the progenitor of Semitic Race to which the Babylonians, Assyrians, Arameans, Arabs and Hebrews belonged. Marr used the term anti-Semitism to make the hatred of Jews seem rational and more scientific.

2.2. Structure and Ingredients of Anti-Semitism

In his book *What Price Prejudice? Christian Antisemitism in America* Frank E. Eakin compares anti-Semitism to a big tree with roots and branches. Anti-Semitism has many roots and many manifestations.

> "Just as an extensive root system comes from all directions to nourish the life of the trunk, so antisemitism derives from many points of causation, which come together in the manifestation of hatred" (Eakin, F.E. 1998: 9)

The four primary ingredients of anti-Semitism are shown in *Price Prejudice! Christian Antisemitism* based on Melvin M Tumin's idea in his book *Antisemitism in the United States*.

> "1. A belief that Jews are different, that they can be identified from non-Jews;
> 2. Some kind of fear of them;
> 3. A desire to keep them at a distance;
> 4. A willingness to discriminate against them, in schools, jobs, housing, social clubs, resorts, and other such places." (Eakin, F.E. 1998: 11)

Abraham H. Foxman, the national director of the Anti-Defamation League (ADL) suggests in his book, *Never Again? The threat of the New Anti-Semitism,* that the world does not seem to have learnt from the tragic consequences of anti-Semitism in World War II. He is convinced that Jewish people are not safe, the threat of anti-Semitism did not pass, and it is even more dangerous due to the modern methods of communication, television, cell phones and internet.

The writer underlines the importance of people's sense of responsibility:

> "Our responsibility is to speak out and to act when tolerance is threatened-and not just in our own backyards or when our own families or friends are in danger, but in all times and places." (Foxman, A H. 2003: 277)

The writer demonstrates the reason why we all have to take actions against anti-Semitism:

> "When our shared culture is polluted by anti-Semitism, racism, ethnic stereotyping, and other forms of bigotry, we all suffer. Particularly in today's dangerous world, it's important for all of us to draw a line in the sand that defines what is acceptable and what is not, and then to defend that line with clarity, consistency, and courage." (Foxman, A H. 2003: 273)

2.3. Assimilation or Dissimilation

According to Foxman assimilation is a "corrosive" effect of anti-Semitism, as it is an unnatural way Jews change their attitude in order to avoid conflicts. It happens automatically, since "pogroms, hate crimes, and Holocaust are not a healthy environment for any people." (Foxman, A. H. 2003:61)

> "Anti-Semitism can affect Jews at least two contradictory ways: it can strengthen their faith or weaken it, depending on personal circumstances, knowledge, and commitment." (Foxman, A. H. 2003:60)

An inevitable consequence of immigrant faith was the transcultural dilemma between the two cultures. It was the search for cultural identity in the meeting point of two cultures. Most of the immigrants choose the way of assimilation "thereby transforming themselves into something like a palimpsest with only a few traces of the original text remaining." (Thiefenthaler, S. L. 1985: 37)

Other immigrants wanted to resist the dominant culture "either by negating the standard norms, values, and codes of the dominant culture or by substituting for the dominant cultural alternative." (Thiefenthaler, S. L. 1985: 37)
There was a transcultural conflict between immigrants' culture, and the dominant culture which provoked a tension between the nations.

Surveys show that anti-Semitic attitudes are declining in the United States, but it did not disappear, in fact it is not a considerate and obvious change. What is visible is that American Jews are abandoning their unique and visibly Jewish features as a result of intermarriage and assimilation.

3. Anti-Semitism in the USA:

Anti-Semitism did not appear in America in such hostile form as in Europe; however, there were some alarming facts that made Jewish American citizens insecure about their lives on the land of freedom.

Robert Michael argues that the first cause of anti-Semitism in the United States was "religious antagonism" (Michael, R. 2005: 5) There were other factors, too like economic jealousy, social competition, political conflict, nativist hostility, and racist ideas.

In American History anti-Semitism generally occurred in times of crises. Anti-Semitism against Jews did not appear in such violent forms as in Europe or Russia, because at the same time, it happened to other social groups and minorities too, and the pressure was divided.
Many early American leaders, like George Washington respected Jews.
In the 19th century however the Jews had no equal social rights due to the Christian origins of America.

Non-Christians had no right to vote in Rhode Island until 1842, North Carolina until 1868, and in New Hampshire until 1871; during the Civil War Jews were accused of supporting the enemy by both sides; Jews were excluded from social circles.

In 1922, Harvard was considering a quota system for Jewish students. Later the idea was dropped but other universities admitted and defended the quota against Jewish students. (For instance medical schools, law firms, banking, insurance, public utilities restricted the entrance of Jews).

3.1. The Leo Frank Case

The Leo Frank case was one of the most frightening incidents in America. On April 26, 1913, Mary Phagan, a thirteen year old girl was found raped and dead in the basement of the pencil factory where Leo Frank was the superintendent. During Leo Frank's trial evidence was introduced suggesting that Frank had many dalliances with girls, and perhaps boys in his employ. After twenty-five days of trial Frank was found guilty not because of solid evidence, but because of public pressure. Governor John Slaton reviewed 10,000 pages of documents and he found that Frank was innocent so he commuted the sentence to life imprisonment. He thought that Frank's innocence would be established later.

On the night of august 16, 1915 some prominent citizens of Marietta, Phagan's hometown, took Frank from the prison in Milledgeville and hung him in the name of justice.

The real murderer was Jim Conley, an African American employee in the pencil factory.

On March 4, 1982, Alonzo Mann confessed that on the night Mary was killed, he saw Jim Conley carrying her dead body. Conley had threatened to kill him if he told it to someone. Although Leo Frank's name was partly cleared, this incident had a great impact on American Jewry. This case generated the formation of the modern Ku Klux Klan, and produced the Jewish Anti-Defamation League.

The Leo Frank case was a miscarriage of justice, and it symbolizes the fears of many people from the South at that time. (After Dinnerstein, L. *The Leo Frank Case* University of Georgia Press, 1999)

The Northern factory owners came to South to reorganize the agricultural economy; the workers resented being exploited by them.

Leo Frank's Jewish origin generated anti-Semitic response to the case. Many of the Georgians believed that Jews just want to take away their money and undermine justice.

3.1.1. The Jews in Atlanta

From the mid 1800s Atlanta was considered one of the most secure places in the South for Jews. (After Herzberg, S. *Strangers within the Gate City: The Jews of Atlanta, 1845-1915.*Philadelphia: Jewish Publication Society of America, 1978)
In 1850 twenty-six Jews lived in Atlanta and they owned more than 10 percent of its retail businesses.
They were immigrants from Europe. Soon, the member of the Jews in Atlanta doubled and grew throughout the following decade.
The Jews in Atlanta were accepted with little prejudice and they had fit into society. Historians argue that prejudice against African Americans protected Jews from discrimination.

The lynching of Leo Frank shattered the sense of security felt by Atlanta's Jews. In spite of their great number in Atlanta, the law could not guarantee a legitimate trial free of prejudice.
Public opinion of gentiles in Georgia was against Jews due to successful businesses founded by Jews. They became excluded from the elite social clubs in Atlanta. Overall, they were tolerated, but also singled out as different.

3.2. Restrictionism

Restrictionism appeared in the late 1800s and became stronger during the Depression. In the decade before World War I. 900,000 immigrants entered the United States. Ten percent of the immigrants were Jewish.
Restrictionists believed that immigrants would take away their jobs and unemployment would be even greater.

The members of the Veterans of Foreign Wars were strongly against foreign immigration together with organisations like Junior Order of United American Mechanics and influential persons like Father Charles E. Coughlin.

3.2.1. Father Charles Coughlin

Father Charles E. Coughlin was a Roman Catholic Priest from Detroit, who opposed immigration with his radio broadcasts and his publication *Social Justice*. Coughlin was able to convince many radio listeners that Jewish bankers caused the Great Depression. He invented a new term: 'international banker' as a new name for the Jews. He suggested that Jews caused the Depression in order to take over control in America. He outlined a Jewish conspiracy.

Nativistic nationalism was another anti-immigrant idea during this period. They wanted to eliminate foreigners from American society for the sake of American citizens. Their fear was at first of material origin but they also feared the different cultures that came to the country.

3.2.2. Wartime Anti-Semitism

Between the two World Wars anti-Semitism "was more widespread and profound than ever before in American history." (Michael, R. 2005: 127)
By the end of the 1930, anti-Semitism was prevalent and openly known in the United States. American anti-Semitism had its peak during World War II.

Coughlin founded the Social Justice Movement. The German American Bund and the American Nazi Movement were formed.

William Dudley, a dangerous anti-Semite, developed the Silver Shirts organisation that counted 100,000 members. They published pamphlets like *What Every Congressman Should Know*. They claimed that there was a Jewish-Communist conspiracy to take over the United States.

September 11. 1941, in Des Moines, Iowa, Charles Lindenberg, the great aviation hero had a speech entitled *"Who are the war Agitators?"* He claimed that Roosevelt Administration, the British and the Jews are pressing America to war. He underlined that Jews have large ownership and influence in business, press, radio, and government.
In fact, Lindenberg was convinced, that no one can win against Hitler's army, and America would only waste life and money in a 'Jewish' war. Lindenberg and many other Americans did not believe that Jews had so terrible lot.

3.3. Henry Ford

Henry Ford could have personified the 'American Hero', as he was a self-made man, upright, successful businessman, religious, strong in character, he brought industrial progress to a whole generation of people; he mass-produced cars and made them affordable and available to Americans.
He gave voice to his anti-Semitic thoughts in articles in the newspaper *Dearborn Independent* that was sponsored by Ford. He published several anti-Semitic books too. (after Baldwin, Neil. *Henry Ford and the Jews: the Mass Production of Hate*. Public Affairs. New York: 2001)
He had a great part in spreading anti-Semitism throughout the American Midwest
He was a pacifist. He spoke vehemently against the warmongers and the international bankers, who he thought were financing the war.

In the *Dearborn Independent* Ford had his own page where he could express his feelings against War, communists, and against the Jews. He also wanted to educate people self-improvement, independent thinking.

Having red the book *The Protocols of the Learned Elders of Zion* Ford became more paranoid with the Jews. The book was the story of a secret meeting held in Switzerland by Jews who wanted to take control of the world, with the goal of enslaving gentiles.

The Dearborn Independent published the Protocols and the International Jew- an anthology of articles.

The Hitler regime honoured Henry Ford with the Verdienstkreutz Deutscher Adler, a German medal for highly appreciated persons.

Ford wrote about Aaron Sapiro, who had farming cooperative and happened to be Jewish. Ford claimed that Jews like Aaron Sapiro live from other farmers' work. Sapiro brought a lawsuit against Ford. At the end, Ford made a public apology, and told that he did not know what had appeared in his newspaper. Everybody knew his apology was not sincere; he just wanted to impress the public.

4. Jewish American Literature

Jewish American writers explored the conflicts between secular society and Jewish tradition. However, the expression Jewish American literature/ writer is problematic since the distinction of writer and Jewish writer may seem anti-Semitic formulation. When we talk about Jewish writers, we cannot avoid mentioning Henry Roth, Saul Bellow, Bernard Malamud, Chaim Potok, and Phillip Roth.
Authors that are more recent are Paul Auster, Michael Chabon, Jonathan Safran Foer, Art Spiegelman. We can mention as common themes, the dilemmas of identity, Holocaust, assimilation, Zionism/Israel, anti-Semitism, New Anti-Semitism.

According to Stephen Wade's book, *Jewish American Literature since 1945* (1999), the creativity of Jewish writers can be explained by internal and external conflicts that produced an immense creative impulse. Wade summarises the two central conflicts that affect the literature of Jewish American writers:

> "1. Jews as an ethnic minority with specific identities to be preserved in a massively saturated popular cultural macro-society. In other words, a new version of cultural assimilation.
> 2. Internecine opposition, in which various versions of Ortodox and Reform Jews have maintained differences. (Wade, S. 1999: 8)

Wade points out that the central characters of the novels and dramas written by Bellow, Malamud, Roth, Miller and others "often find themselves beset by problems of the uprooted, of the place of the intellect and creativity in American society and of the survival of cultural and aesthetic values in a consumer society." (Wade, S. 1999: 9)

5. Arthur Miller

Miller was one of the greatest writers of his time. Miller followed the writing tradition of famous writers like Saul Bellow, Abraham Cahan, Mike Gold, Henry Roth, Isaac Bashevis Singer.

Malcolm Bradbury writes in *The Cambridge Companion to Arthur Miller* reflecting on the writers of that time:

> (…)" I have explored the chastened mood of post-war realism, as novelists responded to the appalling revelations and realisations that followed the war- the news of the Holocaust, the onset of the nuclear age- and the rising sense of unreality that many writers felt as they experienced daily post-war American events. As the nation returned not to Depression but sudden affluence., as a new age of consumerism rose, modern mass-culture spread and society became increasingly suburbanized, the American writer too faced a change of focus, as the ideological and moral perspectives and responsibilities of the thirties yielded to an encounter with the post-war landscape of American and Un-American activities, of superpower status and a culture of individualized personal success." (Bigsby, Ch. 1997: 222)

5.1. Hitler's Quarry

Hitler's Quarry is an essay written by Miller after he graduated from the University of Michigan. It was written in May 1941, before Hitler's plan concerning the annihilation of the Jewish nation was publicly acknowledged by the United States government. In *Hitler's Quarry* Miller draws attention to the persecution of Jews, and blames the United States government's indifference. It seemed that they do not want to help Jewish people escape Nazi persecution.

Miller shows that the plight of the Jewish people is also a threat for all humankind: "Freedom cannot be divided and remain alive. One vein is punctured and the body dies entire." (Miller, A. Hitler's Quarry, 2000: 33)

Hitler's *Quarry remains* relevant because of its universal theme concerning tyranny, exploitation and cruelty. It also shows the basic theoretical background of Miller's fiction, *Focus*.

5.2. Universal Themes in Miller's works

As other Jewish American writers, Miller's works concentrated on general human values, the place of the individual in a gigantic and hostile society, anti-Semitism. According to Wade, Miller chose these important and complex themes "with a sense of innovation and experiment, juxtaposing the pains of the interior life with the visible injustice and barbarities of the Jewish experience in modern times." (Wade, S. 1999: 96)

> "In *After the Fall* (1964), *Incident at Vichy* (1964), *The Prince* (1968), *Playing for Time* (1980), *Danger Memory* (1968), *Broken Glass* (1994) he has interwoven the subjects of anti-Semitism, Holocaust experience and urban Jewish-American generational change, with a central narrative drive towards the question of what is to be Jewish." (Wade, S. 1999: 97)

The theme of these plays reflected Miller's preoccupation with the problem of evil and the responsibility of the individual. "His dramatic subjects have always been close to the moral arena of decisions, dilemmas and crises of conformity and individuality". (Wade, S. 1999: 97)

5.3. A Brief Chronology of Arthur Miller's Life and Works

The following chronology of important dates is taken from Robert W. Corrigan's *Arthur Miller, A collection of Critical Essays* and completed after ibiblio.org

1905	Arthur Miller born in New York City.
1936	Attends University of Michigan. First Play, *Honors at Dawn*, produced. Wins Avery Hopwood Award.
1938	*No Villain* wins Hopwood Award and Theatre Guild Prize. Miller graduates from Michigan and joins the Federal Theatre Project.
1940	Marries Mary Slatery.
1944	*The Man Who Had All the Luck*- his first Broadway production. *Situation Normal* published.
1945	His novel, *Focus* published.
1947	*All My Sons* produced.
1949	*Death of a Salesman* produced and wins Pulitzer Prize.
1950	His adaptation of Ibsen's *An Enemy of the People* produced.
1953	*The Crucible* produced.
1955	*A Memory of Two Mondays* and the one-act version of *A View from the Bridge* produced.
1956	He appears before House Un-American Activities Committee and refuses to inform on others. The revised two-act version of *A View from the Bridge* produced in London. Receives an honorary doctorate from the University of Michigan. Divorces Mary Slatery and Marries Marilyn Monroe.
1957	Convicted for contempt of Congress. *Collected Plays* published.
1958	Contempt conviction reversed. Elected to the National Institute of Arts and Letters.
1960	He and Marilyn Monroe divorced.
1961	*The Misfits* released.
1962	Marries Inge Morath? Daughter Rebecca born.
1964	*After the Fall* is premiere production of Repertory Theatre of Lincoln Centre. *Incident at Vichy* also produced there.

1965	Elected International President of P.E.N. (Poets, Essayists, and Novelists).
1967	*I Don't Need You Any More*, a collection of short stories, published.
1968	*The Prince* produced.
1972	First sound recording of The Crucible.
1973	Television production of Incident at Vichy, on PBS.
1974	Television production of After the Fall, on NBC.
1978	*The Theatre Essays of Arthur Miller*, edited by Robert A. Martin published. Fame (film) appears on NBC. Belgian National Theatre does 25th anniversary production of The Crucible.
1981	The second volume of Arthur Miller's Collected Plays published.
1983	Directs Death of a Salesman at the People's Art Theatre in Beijing, the People's Republic of China.
1984	*Salesman in Beijing* is published. Elegy and Some Kind are published under the new title *Two-Way Mirror*. Miller receives Kennedy Centre Honours for his lifetime achievement.
1985	*Death of a Salesman* with Dustin Hoffman airs on CBS to an audience of 25 million.
1987	Television production of *All My Sons*, on PBS.
1990	Television production of *An Enemy of the People*, on PBS.
1991	Receives Mellon Bank Award for lifetime achievement in the humanities.
1994	*Broken Glass* premiers. Interviewed on The Charley Rose Show, PBS.
1995	Receives William Inge Festival Award for distinguished achievement in American theatre.
1996	Receives the Edward Albee Last Frontier Playwright Award.
1997	The Crucible (film with Daniel Day Lewis) opens. BBC television production of Broken Glass.
1998	*Mr. Peter's Connections* premiers. Major revival of *A View From the Bridge* wins two Tony Awards. Is named as the Distinguished Inaugural Senior Fellow of the American Academy in Berlin.
1999	*Death of a Salesman* revived on Broadway for the play's 50th anniversary, and wins Tony for Best Revival of a Play.

2000   There are major 85th birthday celebrations for Miller held at University of Michigan and at the Arthur Miller Center at UEA, England. *Echoes Down the Corridor* is published (collected essays from 1944-2000).

2001   Miller is awarded a NEH Fellowship and the John H. Finley Award for Exemplary Service to New York City.

2002   New York City revivals of *The Man Who Had All the Luck* and *The Crucible*. Inge Morath dies. Premier of *Resurrection Blues*. Awarded the International Spanish Award: Premio Principe de Asturias de las Letras.

2003   Awarded the Jerusalem Prize

2004   New York City revival of *After the Fall*. Premier of *Finishing the Picture*.

2005   Miller dies of heart failure in his Connecticut home on 10 February. Memorial Services held in Roxbury and NY.

6. Focus

The novel appeared in 1945 in 90,000 copies. Miller was thirty when he wrote the novel and he was at the beginning of his career.

Malcolm Bradbury points out in *The Cambridge Companion to Arthur Miller* that *Focus* like many other important novels belongs to the "new surge of culturally central Jewish-American fiction which would make its mark over the immediate post-war years." (Bigsby, C. 1997: 215) Bigsby mentions Saul Bellow's *Dangling Man* (1944), *The Victim* (1947), Isaac Rosenfeld's *Passage from Home* (1946), Isaac Bashevis Singer's *Gimpel the Fool* (1947), Delmore Schwartz's *The World is a Wedding* (1948), Norman Mailer's *The Barbary Shore* (1951), Bernard Malamud's *The Natural* (1952). These novels have a common feature, the main character: "The Jewish hero- introvert, underground man, urban wanderer, outsider, victim, survivor, schlemiel" (Bigsby, C. 1997:216)

After the failure of his play, *The Man Who Had All the Luck*, which ran for only four days Miller, turned away from playwriting and wrote a novel, *Focus*. Malcolm Bradbury writes about *Focus*:

> "It was written in wartime Manhattan where Miller- who has been turned down for military service as a result of an injury, and worked in the New York Naval Yard repairing ships- felt displaced, uneasy, and politically indignant about the mood on the home front. At the yard, he was witness to a climate of anti-Semitism and incipient Fascism."(Bigsby, C. 1999: 217)

According to Bradbury *Focus* is "a novel about the growing racial and anti-semitic tension" in America during the War. The subject of the novel is anti-Semitism but it also points out the "irrational hatred directed towards practically any racial minority" (Hogan, R. 1967: 15)

> "Americans of Arthur Miller's time endured the Great Depression and two world wars. And yet this toughest of generations was routinely moved to tears by Miller's dramas about the pain of ordinary American life. After

the curtain dropped, there would often be stunned silence in the theatre, and then the sound of sobbing." (Gottfried, M. 2003)

Malcolm Bradbury suggests that Miller's *Focus* is prominent among the other post-war Jewish novels of the time with its "explicitness and directness". (Bigsby, C. 1999: 222)

Focus is one of the first books that directly confront American anti-Semitism. It is about men's inhumanity to men.
The scene is New York City; the time is during the war.
As World War II draws to a close, anti-Semitism is alive in Brooklyn, New York. This period is marked by morally aggressive acts against Jews, for instance many social institutions, companies, or shops had a note on the entrance telling "No dogs, or Jews allowed". The discrimination happened to African Americans, and other ethnical minorities, too. Words like 'kike', or 'dirty Jew' were often herd even from children, who learned this attitude from their parents. All seemed natural, obvious. The tension grew due to the financial difficulties caused by Depression, when

6.1. Lawrence Newman

The main character; Lawrence Newman is a typical representative of an indifferent, passive man, who has anti-Semitic feelings. He detests Jewish people without knowing the real reason of his feelings. He is a narrow-minded employee in a big company where racial prejudice is common. Newman is indifferent to the racism around him in the neighbourhood, too. He has no wife and he lives with his invalid mother. He is a lonely person and he feels superior to his neighbours. The conflict appears when he is mistaken for a Jew and everybody wants him out of the neighbourhood. Throughout the novel Newman falls in love, gets married and because of a pair of glasses, he looses his former identity. His existence is in danger and at the end, he only finds one friendly, honest person by him, a Jew. His life becomes a struggle for dignity and survival being the victim of religious and racial persecution..

Some of his comments on Jews:
> -"There's a lot of reasons why people don't like Jews. They have no principles, for one thing."
> -"No principles."
> -"Yes. In business, you'll find them cheating and take advantage, for instance.
> -That's something that people. . . . "
> -"Let me understand. You're talking about me now?"
> -"Well, no, not you, but. . . ."
> -"I ain't interested in other people, Mr. Newman. I live on this block and there ain't another Jew on this block but me and my family. Did I ever cheat you in business?"
> -"That's not the point. You. . ."
> -"It's not what you've done, it' what others of your people have done."
> (Miller, A. 2002: 165)

The novel begins with a dream. Lawrence Newman is dreaming about a carousel in an amusement park. It is a deserted place, with no people around but Newman has a strange feeling that something evil is going on:

> "He new that underneath, below the ground, there was a gigantic machine operating: a factory, he realised. Something was being manufactured beneath the carousel, and trying to imagine what it was he grew frightened." (Miller, A. 2002: 1)

Miller's novel shows the main character's moral improvement.
At the beginning of the novel Lawrence Newman works at a large business enterprise as a personal manager. His job is to refuse Jewish-looking applicants. He is a typical functionary whose only joy in life is his success in his job. His highest dream is to find the perfect employee.

Newman is not a hero. He is just an average middle-aged man who takes care of his car and his sick mother. We might say that at the beginning of the novel Newman is like Willy Loman from The Death of a Salesman, insignificant, full of faults in his personality.

"Nothing in the novel is more successfully or more movingly depicted than Newman's essential littleness, meekness' and hesitancy." Wellard's opinion is that Miller chose Newman as his main character in order to alienate the reader from the character to underline the main issue, namely anti-Semitism Wellard calls this technique the Brechtian "estrangement" (Wellard, D. 1961:19)

6.2. The Spectacles:

Being a member of a segregated group makes a man see life better. Dennis Wellard says in his book about Newman:

> "When he is forced into buying them it is the spectacles that accentuate his Jewish appearance and precipitate his victimisation by a world that he can at least see more clearly."(Wellard, D.1961: 16)

This way the spectacles become more important, because from that date Newman's evolution begins. The process of change in his personality began a little bit earlier, when he realised that he could not see well.

> "But lately it had become a terrorising experience to sit in full view of the stenographers. For when he raised his eyes he could see nothing through the glass. At this moment, someone might be beckoning to him out there, and getting no response. His days were spent in walking up and down the rows of desks as though on errands of importance, while in fact he was desperately trying to be where he could be summoned by voice." (Miller, A. 2002: 14)

The inevitable happens. He makes a big mistake as he hires a Jewish typist, Miss Kapp, whose "name must be Kapinski or something" as Newman's boss Mr. Gargan says.
It is a very unpleasant situation, when Newman is questioned. He is insecure and ashamed about what he did. He is inferior and treated as a child. All his life he was afraid of the situations like that and he was trying to avoid them not being able to treat the feeling well.
Of course, the scene is absurd; when Newman is ashamed for the wrong reason, that he hired a Jewish person. This would not have been a mistake in a healthy society. Newman does not notice the faults of the system that he is part of. He only wants to save his reputation.

The twisted situation gets odder when his boss explains why Miss Kapp's presence is so unpleasant:

> "It throws the whole office off, having somebody like that around. The girls spend half their time in the rest room talking about her. And you know the job it is getting rid of them." (Miller, A. 2002: 17)

Mr. Gargan cannot understand why Newman does not want to get a pair of spectacles if he does not see well. Later it becomes clear that Newman's threats were realistic. You do not have to be a Jew if you look like a Jew. You have to bear the consequences.

Most of the time he feels miserable, but especially at the optometrist's office. It is obvious that he wants to escape as soon as he can.

His mother's short remark, "you almost look like a Jew", makes his fear grow, and at the same time, we get to know that Newman cannot be sincere even with his mother. As her reaction makes clear that, she has a worse personality than Newman, that she has anti-Semitic feelings, too.

6.2.1. The Spectacles, Device for Focusing

There is another point we begin to think about the importance of the glasses. That is the title.

There is a close connection between the glasses and focusing. As Dennis Wellard says:

> "Focusing implies a narrowing of the vision, however, a concentration on a more limited area, and although this justifies the pattern of the novel- the tension increasing as the vision narrows- it does lead to some distortion of perspective."(Wellard, D. 1961: 16)

6.3. Aleese!

Awakened from his dream Newman talked himself out of helping a woman in trouble. She was "Spanish. Probably Puerto Rican" (Miller, A 2002: 2). The fact, that the woman was not a white American, made him decide not to help her. Nobody else did. Newman keeps hearing this agitating voice from time to time. He knows that he did not behave right.

In chapter fourteen, he is awakened again by a noise from the street. He had gone through many things since the first cry, he experienced anti-Semitism on his own skin and he changed. He thought that Mr. Finkelstein was being beaten up. He knew that he would act otherwise he did at the first time. He knows what to do now:"Simply call the police and not have to leave the house…" (Miller, A. 2002: 134) He has changed, but not enough yet.

By the penultimate chapter, he is almost a new man. He is able to see that something is not right in the way things are. He relives the moments he heard the woman screaming:

> "Aleese! She could have been murdered, clubbed to death out here that night. No one would have dared outdoors to help, to even say she was a human being. Because all of them watching from their windows knew she was not white" (Miller, A. 2002: 174)

6.4. The Company

According to Leonard Moss, both the corporation and Newman's neighbourhood have a very important part in the novel. They are "monolithic institutions from which the wayward are cast." (Moss, L. 1967: 37)

He had his own desk in his own office on the sixteenth floor of a skyscraper that had a large Gothic entrance. Moreover, this is only one of the many buildings the corporation had all over the world. The huge size of this institution only makes Newman appear smaller though he desperately tries to convince himself that he is irreplaceable. He survived the Depression, so he can be proud of himself, but he has reasons not to feel secure totally, because America is still going through rough times.

We get to know Mr.Gargan, Newman's boss, as he was mentioned before, and Mr. George Lorsch, the vice president of the company. Mr Lorsch was the one who made specifications about the persons who can be hired in the company. In addition, Mr. Lorsch is the one who does not want Newman to be seen at the company. He and M. Gargan want him to change office with Hogan whom Newman does not respect at all. Newman is proud enough not to accept this unfair offer.

The scene between him and his boss is very tense. Newman feels driven to the wall so he acts unexpected. Even he himself is surprised. He feels it unfair that he must leave his office, because he is not Jewish. He does not see the absurdity in the fact that somebody is not hired, because he or she is Jewish.

It is funny though that Newman's mother thinks in a way that he has a friendly relationship with Mr. Gargan.

6.5. The Other Company

Looking for job becomes another lesson for Newman.
Miller writes in chapter ten about Mr. Finkelstein that he" was still a young man, but as a Jew he was very old." (Miller, A. 2002: 75)
Mr. Newman is quite a good clerk. Looking like a Jew, he is not wanted in most of the companies in Manhattan. It became clear that Akron Corporation was looking for a man like him, but he could not do anything. He could not possibly explain that he has nothing to do with Jews, because in situations like these, things remain unsaid.

Meyers-Peterson Corporation was a different kind of company. The receptionist was a Jewess. This made Newman believe he had a chance. However, a familiar face interviews him. It is Gertrude Hart, the woman he refused to hire because of her Jewish appearance. The scene is tense again, as it was when they met for the first time. Newman is more insecure now. "You don't need your experience for this place. They hire anybody in this place. All they do is ask if you are a citizen. Jews, niggers, wops, anybody." (Miller, A. 2002: 82)
Gertrude is in advantage, and Newman is grateful to her, as she does not take her advantage of the opportunity. In fact she was in an advantage at the first time, too as she happed to be a very desirable woman, the same person Newman was dreaming of.
Newman does not see the twist in the situation, that he is an employee at a Jewish company. His anti-Semitic feelings do not occur in a conscious level. He does not think about these things, he lets his subconscious prejudices act as if they were normal.

6.6. The Dream Woman

Gertrude Hart is a woman who makes most men excited.
"Gertrude Hart, age thirty-six, three years of high school. Unmarried, Episcopalian. Born in Rochester, New York." (Miller, A. 2002: 29)
She smells of perfume. She knows how to dress in order to look everything but ordinary. Moreover, she is confident. She is not afraid to tell what she thinks. At first, we think that her personality is created to be more human than Newman's is. Then we find out that, as Newman's character changes for the better, Gertrude can only reveal hers. She does not change but as we see her better, we cannot but despise her and feel pity about Newman.

Malcolm Bradbury's opinion is that "the only well shaped character in the novel is Newman. The other characters in the novel are shadowy and deceptive, and shift in the meaning and emphasis according to Newman's perception of them: his changing focus." (Bigsby, C. 1997: 21)

Newman's feelings towards Gertrude are filtered through his anti- Semitic thoughts. When they meet for the first time, Newman is sure that she is Jewish. Although he knows she is the woman he dreamt of, he is afraid of her. „In first focus, he sees her as Jewish and erotically dangerous; later she is seen as gentile and desirable."
(Bigsby, C. 1997: 221) He wants to get rid of her in the company but he continues to think about her. When they meet for the second time and it becomes clear that she is a Gentile, Newman feels relief and he is ashamed.

In the novel good things and bad things happen to Newman.
He is not in control of his life; he is a toy in the hands of the surrounding society.
As for Gertrude, she is a strong and conscious woman. From the very beginning, she knows what she wants and she does not select among tools.

6.6.1. The Demonized Woman

What is obvious for the reader is that she does not really love Newman, she just needs him. She wants to live the life of an average American housewife, not to be obliged to work, to have fancy clothes, some friendly neighbour, and a bit of entertainment from time to time.

The scene when Newman proposes to Gert is a typical presentation of how some women can manipulate men simply by using their feminine power of seduction. She is teasing the man:" I was just thinking something silly." (Miller, A. 2002: 101) In addition, of course Newman walks into the trap asking- what? "What I would say if you asked me to marry you." (Miller, A. 2002: 101) This is the moment when the reader takes Newman's side and wants him to get out of there to find a decent woman.

Newman marries Gertrude thinking that she is leading him towards higher goals, as she sees potential in him. Newman is eager to believe that he is a fine young man that Gertrude suggests to be, and still he is terrified by the thought that this beautiful dream with this exceptional woman would suddenly end. He is an easy prey.

When time passes and Newman begins to see with the eyes of unrightfully hated ones the truths about his wife begin to appear. "She is certainly a story- teller, who fictionalizes freely about her own identity and her past." (Bigsby, C. 1997: 221) Newman is surprised each time a lie clears up. A process has begun and the two of them cannot find each other any more. Newman takes a few desperate efforts to make Gertrude understand what he has found out, that every man deserves to be free and live wherever he wants, that no man is above the other, but the woman blames him for everything.

At the end, when Newman and Mr. Finkelstein are beaten up, and Gertrude desperately wants to explain Fred the "misunderstanding" instead of calling the police, Gertrude's metamorphoses becomes complete in Newman's eyes. She becomes a dirty woman, despicable and ugly.

6.7. Finkelstein, the Jew

He is one of the major causes of Newman's change. A simple man, tortured by history, society, neighbourhood and life.
He is the other perspective in the novel. A simple, uneducated man, capable of facing the whole world.
According to Malcolm Bradbury, Finkelstein is the only other character in the novel who is thoroughly shaped and whose point of view is shown to the reader in detail. His person becomes the opponent to Newman.

> "His story is separately told, a counterpoint to Newman's, and he becomes the formidable 'other,' the key object of attention and responsibility in the book." (Bigsby, C. 1997: 221)

Newman always bought his daily paper across the street at Mr. Finkelstein's shop. That was a natural and logical habit of his, as it was close. Fred and his anti-Semite friends change this routine by sabotaging Finkelstein's shop. Although they do not physically hurt the old man, their act is aggressive and mean.
Newman feels that something is not right but in that moment he concentrates only on his frustration of not being popular, and the odd feeling of being obligated to change his attitude towards the Jewish man.
Surprisingly he is angry with Finkelstein. He feels that the problem is Finkelstein's presence, that the problem is his existence. The situation gets worse when Finkelstein's father appears. He thinks that it is true what Frank and his fellowmen are saying, that Jews are going to invade the neighbourhood and they will cause problem.
In the scene, when Newman wants to buy his newspaper, the reader gets the feeling that the only adult present is Mr. Finkelstein. The others act like mean adolescents.

6.8. Mr. Finkelstein

It is interesting, that we see Finkelstein from different perspectives. Newman is indifferent at first; he just does not want to get in trouble. Frank and the other anti-Semitists hate him and detest him, and they want to get rid of him. Gertrude is afraid of him and the consequences of being treated alike.

Leonard Moss summarises Newman's personality:

> "Somewhat enlightened and greatly fortified, Newman begins to realise the consequences of anti-Semitism from the viewpoint of a Jew. The insults that he suffers after his new eyeglasses give his face a "Jewish" appearance extend his awareness. Finally, his vision focuses upon the individual rather than upon an illusory abstraction; he can sympathize with Finkelstein's furious refusal to be deprived of a personal identity: "looking at Finkelstein now, Newman saw that he had not really hated him, ...he had passed this man each morning with the knowledge that he had him the propensity for acting as Jews were supposed to; cheat, or be dirty, or loud.(...)Newman's history illustrates the conclusion that racial intolerance, when raised to a system of belief, frustrates this "compulsion" in the person who practices it as well as in the person victimized by it." (Moss, L. 1967: 35- 36)

Using Newman as a protagonist, Miller manages to show that in crucial questions like racism and anti-Semitism no one can be impartial.

Focus is not only the novel of Newman's change from an anti-Semite to a human being but it is also the novel of Mr Finkelstein's transformation in Newman's eyes. First Newman sees a Jew, a member of a despised 'race', than gradually, as he starts thinking, he can see the real person.

Through this novel, Miller suggests that stereotypes can be defeated with intelligence.

7. Conclusion

Anti-Semitism is an immensely damaging form of ethnic and religious intolerance, with consequences for everyone.
The roots of anti-Semitism can be traced back to ancient times. Some historians say that it is as old as humankind is.
The thesis concentrates on American anti-Semitism presented in Arthur Miller's *Focus*.

Anti-Semitism in the United States was not present with the same intensity as in Europe, but it still had serious consequences in the past and it continues to influence present times too.
The Leo Frank case is considered one of the most severe consequences of American anti-Semitism. It produced a public hysteria and arbitrary judgement, that caused an innocent man's death.
The case generated the formation of the modern Klu Klux Klan and the Jewish Anti-Defamation League. It had a very destructive effect on American Jewry, making them insecure about their future.

The appearance of Restrictionism helped anti-Semitism deepen in the minds of the inhabitants of the United States.
The evolution of anti-Semitism is helped a great deal by persons like Charles E. Coughlin. He attracted a huge number of listeners with his radio broadcasts. His listeners believed his words, and hostile attitude against Jews became more and more obvious.
Henry Ford was also a destructive person from the point of spreading anti-Semitism around the country.

The effect of the Great Depression was another factor that made anti-Semitism stronger in the United States, as people believed it was caused by Jewish bankers who were part of a great conspiracy to take over control in America.

Anti-Semitism had its peak during World War II, when Americans feared Jewish refugees. Most of the people believed that there were German spies among the refugees.
The Evian Conference was President Roosevelt's unsuccessful attempt to solve the problem of the refugees. American attitude towards the suffering of Jewish people remained indifferent.

Jewish American literature presented the conflict between secular society and Jewish tradition. Anti-Semitism is one of the major themes writers dealt with.

Arthur Miller's novel *Focus* is one of the most outstanding works on anti-Semitism. As other Jewish American writers, Miller is concerned about the future of the American Jews.
The novel presents the moral crises caused by the recognition of the falseness of anti-Semitism. An unusual point of view is shown by the writer, when the main character is faced with violent anti-Semitism though he is not Jewish, only others consider him one, due to his glasses. This way, the change of Newman's identity gets in the focus of the novel. His place in society changes completely.
From a settled, calm, white American he changes into a Jew, the enemy of the people.

His mind goes through a change, he becomes a new person, a better one, but he looses his former life and chooses to think by himself in a hostile world in which so many people wanted to influence others.

Focus is an outstanding piece of writing in Miller's life. It is his only novel. The first, that openly presents American anti-Semitism. It reflects American people's attitude towards Jewish people during the war.

8. Pedagogical Implications

As a parent, I want my children to be free of preconceptions as much as I want them to be healthy, happy, independent, a complete personality. As a teacher I want my students to have the opportunity to meet the truths, I want them to form their own ideas about life and history, about human values, about things that are really important. For this reason, it is very important that children meet real values at school in the case they have anti-Semitic parents.

It would be essential not to have teachers who have not clear opinion and deep knowledge on history because school should be the source of pure knowledge, real values. It should not only teach it should educate.

The International school for Holocaust Studies website has a conclusion in his introduction that could be universal in schools too:

> "During the Weimar Republic, the Nazis began assaulting Jews with words. Following their rise to power in 1933, verbal attacks were gradually followed by economic discrimination and later by physical destruction. It is important Auschwitz, but rather it began with the deionization of Jews: anti- crematoria of January, the day on which we mark the liberation of Auschwitz, we must honor not only the memory of human beings who were murdered simply because of their race, but we must also confront how the Holocaust has become part of contemporary antisemitic slogans and strongly combat antisemitism in our midst.
> By fighting contemporary antisemitism and other forms of xenophobia in our respective schools, we safeguard Holocaust memory and thereby put its universal lessons into practice."(http://www.yadvashem.org 20. márc. 2008.)

History has taught us a very painful lesson on anti-Semitism, and the consequences of this hatred. In spite of this in many European countries anti-Semitism has frighteningly risen. Jewish cemeteries have been vandalized in Budapest, London, and Manchester in 2005. New neo Nazi groups appeared. Violence has grown even in primary schools and the teacher remains inert. Still, it is the teacher's responsibility to retain values and to try to influence them in a good way.

A foreign language teacher's major aim is to teach the language. However, teachers can use their class to concentrate on major problems like anti-Semitism. Pupils have a basic knowledge about the Holocaust from their history lessons but they do not necessarily know the origin of anti-Semitism, the roots of this ancient phobia.

In order to teach the history of anti-Semitism we need a longer teaching period. It has to be presented step by step through various teaching devices involving other classes too if it is possible, for instance the History class, Ethics, or Class- master's class. The theme makes it possible to have as many speaking exercises as we want or the time allows. We can also use the theme to know our students better, asking about their feelings towards their gipsy classmates, or asking gips children about their feelings when they are treated disrespectfully because of their origin.

The next step is to introduce Arthur Miller in our curriculum. Miller's life can be interesting to the pupils from many perspectives. (His marriage to Marilyn Monroe; the rough times in the McCarthy area).
Teaching Miller, we cannot forget to talk about his other major works, like 'The Crucible' or 'The Death of a Salesman'.

'Focus' is a very good choice in order to teach a novel because it is a classic novel that is relevant to today's students too. It has a strong main idea, it is well written, its characters are well shaped, the plot is interesting, and the dialogues are full of tension. It's theme is universal so it can be used in other classes too.

Teachers are constantly facing the situation of having too much to teach but in addition, little time so we have to organise our lessons in the most favourable way.

All students have to read the novel. The most favourable is to read in English, but if it is too difficult for them, they can read it in their mother tongue. They should use a reading journal because it makes reading more effective. The process of using the journal has to be with the careful guidance of the teacher who underlines the most important parts, points out the characters they must pay attention to. It is favourable for the students to have the opportunity to talk to their teacher about the novel if they have difficulties in understanding the novel.

Before starting to talk about anti-Semitism the teacher should gather the historical data, pictures and a list of works about the theme for the case that someone is interested and wants to have deeper knowledge in the theme. In an additional class pupils can watch 'Schindler's List'.

Video list

-Broken Glass (1966), directed by David Thacker;
-Cabaret (1972), directed by Bob Fosse;
-A Call to Remember (1997), directed by Jack Bender;
-Chariots of Fire (1981), directed by Hugy Hudson;
-Charlie Grant's War (1980), directed by Martin Lavut;
-The Chosen (1980), Jeremy Paul Kagan
-Cold Days (1966), directed by Kovács András
-Crossfire (1947), directed by Edward Dmytryk
-Dark Lullabies (1985), directed by Irene Angelico, Abbey Neidik;
A lot of pictures, historical data, and documents can be found on 'A Teacher's Guide to Holocaust' website on the internet.

8.1. Lesson Plan 1

Aim: The aim of the first class is to present the students the plan concerning the theme. It is important for the students to know the amount of the material they are going to learn, the topic they are going to focus on. The second aim is to arouse the student's interest towards the topic, and to know their opinion about it.

1. Speaking. (Maximum 25 minutes) In speaking activities, the most important is to create an atmosphere where pupils can express their thoughts freely. The teacher guides the conversation and helps if it is stuck. It is not the aim to correct all the mistakes pupils make but the teacher must not forget that the theme is a device to use the English language and to teach it.

   The questions:
   - What is anti-Semitism?
   - Do you know a Jewish person?
   - Are Jewish people 'different'?
   - What is your opinion about neo natzi persons?
   - What do you know about the Holocaust?
   - Have you ever seen a film on anti-Semitism? Can you tell us about it? Etc.

2. Group work. (Maximum 10 minutes). We make three or for groups. Each group gets three words and they have to make definitions to the words. The words: anti-Semitism; Jewish; Nazi; Holocaust; preconception; death camp; hatred; etc. When the definitions are ready, one student from each group reads a definition and the pupils from the other groups try to find out the word.

3. Writing (Maximum 5 minutes) The groups have to find the real definitions in an English-English dictionary.

Homework: Pupils have to look for information on the internet about anti-Semitism. (The origin of anti-Semitism). They have to write a few sentences about what they found mentioning precisely where they fund it.

8.2. Lesson Plan 2

Warm up :(Maximum 10 minutes) Revision. What do pupils remember from the last class? Helping questions: What did we speak about last time? What is anti-Semitism? What do we call 'race'? What does 'Holocaust' mean? Etc.

Checking of the homework: (Maximum 15 minutes) If it is a small group with approximately 10-12 students we can listen each student one by one. It is important to know if everyone made the homework and if they bothered with the exercise, we must make time to check it and correct the mistakes.

Reading: (Maximum 15 minutes) The teacher has to find a summary on the history of anti-Semitism. The text should be suitable for the students' level of knowledge or it can be on a relatively higher level for the sake of learning the language.

Homework: Te students have to summarise the text mentioned above in 60 words.

8.3. Lesson Plan 3

Checking of the homework: (Maximum 10 minutes) It may be useful to have a list of the pupils and always register if someone has not done the homework.

Listening: (Maximum 15 minutes) The teacher has to find a recording that can be used for this purpose. The theme can be widened; Martin Luther King's famous speech can also be used.

Writing: (Maximum 10 minutes) We can use the tape script and make a 'fill in the gaps' exercise. To make the exercise a little bit more difficult we can leave out more than one word.

Group work: (Maximum 10 minutes) The students work in small groups made of three or four students. The students have to write letters for each other about their experiences on anti-Semitism. The groups change the letters and read the letters.

8.4. Lesson Plan 4

Speaking: The fourth class deals with Arthur Miller's life. In the introduction, the teacher talks about American history. The reaction of the American people to the World Wars. The hostile behaviour Jewish people met during World War 2. Arthur Miller's life can be found in almost every editions of his works but it is more effective if the teacher talks about it. Pupils can talk about what they already know about Miller. They might have met his name when they looked for information about anti-Semitism, or they might have heard about his marriage to Marilyn Monroe. The teacher should bring some pictures about Miller's life.

The teacher must talk about Miller's plays too. 'The Crucible' and 'The Death of a Salesman' cannot be left out teaching Miller. It might be useful to talk about the difference between the two genres, the play and the novel.

Homework: The pupils have to choose their favourite chapter from 'Focus' and make a summary of it in a few sentences. The pupils have to bring their reading journals that they used during the reading of the novel for the next class.

8.5. Lesson Plan 5

Checking of the homework: (Maximum 15 minutes) Although the reading journals must be continuously checked and corrected by the teacher, it is necessary to have a class where pupils can see what their classmates have done. It is also interesting to find out which chapter is the students' favourite. This way the teacher can choose the best part for them for further work.

Reading: (Maximum 20 minutes) The pupils read aloud the part they liked the best from their chapter chosen before. The students must focus on right pronunciation, intonation, and expressivity. If the chosen part happens to be a dialogue, they can red it in pair.

Homework: The exercise needs some previous guidance. The pupils have to analyse a character from the novel in 100 words.

8.6. Lesson Plan 6

After checking the homework, the students get a new exercise, which concentrates on the characters and their relationship with each other. We have the four major characters and six interesting choices. Newman's feelings towards Gert; Gert' feelings towards Newman; Gert's attitude towards Mr. Finkelstein; Mr Finkelstein's feelings towards Gert and Fred. Fred's attitude towards Newman; Newman's Feelings to Mr Finkelstein and back.

The pupils work in pairs and they look for sentences in the novel referring to the relationship they chose. After that, they read it aloud. First Newman's Feelings to Gert, then Gert's feelings to Newman, and so on.

Te class can talk about how would they change the story, what would they do otherwise if they were in the place of the writer.

At the end of this class or in a separate lesson, the pupils should tell what they learnt during this theme. We can view the teaching period successful in the case that students learn new words, some historical facts about anti-Semitism and they also start thinking about their own feelings towards other people.

Works cited:

Reference Works:

Baldwin, Neil (2001) *Henry Ford and the Jews: the Mass Production of Hate*. New York: Public Affairs

Bigsby, Christopher (1997) *The Cambridge Companion to Arthur Miller*. United Kingdom: Cambridge University Press

Corrigan, Robert W. (1969) *Arthur Miller A Collection of Critical Essays*. NewYork: Prentice-Hall,Inc.

Crandell, George W. (2000) Arthur Miller's Unheard Plea for Jewish Refugees: "Hitler's Quarry". ANQ, Wntr 2000 v13 i1 p33, University Press of Kentucky

Dinnerstein, Leonard (1999*) The Leo Frank Case*. Atlanta: University of Georgia Press

Dinnerstein, Leonard (1994) *Antisemitism in America*. New York: Oxford University Press, Inc.

Eakin Frank E. (1998) *What price Prejudice? Antisemitism in America*. New Jersey: Paulist Press

Foxman, Abraham H. (2003) Never Again? The Threat of the New Anty-Semitism. New York:HarperCollins Publishers, Inc.

Gottfried, Martin (2003) Arthur Miller's Words and Deed. Da Capo Press, Lit. Pc Document

Herzberg, Steven (1978) *Strangers within the Gate City: The Jews of Atlanta, 1845-1915*. Philadelphia: Jewish Publication Society of America

Hogan, Robert. (1967) *Arthur Miller*. Minneapolis: University of Minnesota Press

Michael, Robert. (2005) *A Concise History of American Antisemitism*. New York: Rowman&Litlefeld

Miller, Arthur. (2002) *Focus*. London: Methuen Publishing LTD

Moss, Leonard. (1967) *Arthur Miller*. NewYork: Twain Publishers Inc.

Robertson, Ritchie (1999) *The Jewish Question in German Literature, 1749-1939*. Oxford University Press

Thiefenthaler, Sepp L.(1985) *The Search for Cultural Identity: Jewish-American Immigrant Autobiographies as Agents of Ethnicity*. The Society for the Study of the Multy-Ethnic literature of the United States. Melius, Vol. 12, Nr.4, European Perspectives

Wade, Stephen (1999) Jewish American Literature since 1945: An Introduction. Edinburgh: Edinburgh University Press

Wellard, Dennis. (1961) *Arthur Miller*. London: Oliver and Boyd LTD

Internet Resources:

http://www.yadvashem.org 20. márc. 2008.

Contents

1. Introduction 1
2. Anti-Semitism 3
    2.1. The Word and its Origin 3
    2.2. Structure and Ingredients of Anti-Semitism 4
    2.3. Assimilation or Dissimilation 5
3. Anti-Semitism in the United States 7
    3.1. The Leo Frank Case 8
        3.1.1. The Jews in Atlanta 9
    3.2. Restrictionism 9
        3.2.1. Father Charles Coughlin 10
    3.3. Henry Ford 11
4. Jewish American Literature 13
5. Arthur Miller 14
    5.1. Hitler's Quarry 14
    5.2. Universal Themes in Miller's Works 15
    5.3. A Brief Chronology of Arthur Miller's Life and Works 16
6. Focus 19
    6.1. Lawrence Newman 20
    6.2. The Spectacles 23
        6.2.1 The Spectacles, Device for Focusing 24
    6.3. Aleese! 25
    6.4. The Company 26
    6.5. The Other Company 27
    6.6. The Dream Woman 28
        6.6.1 The Demonized Woman 29
    6.7. Finkelstein, the Jew 30
    6.8. Mr. Finkelstein 31
7. Conclusion 32
8. Pedagogical Implications 34
    8.1. Lesson Plan 1 37

    8.2. Lesson Plan 2 38

    8.3. Lesson Plan 3 39

    8.4. Lesson Plan 4 39

    8.5. Lesson Plan 5 40

    8.6. Lesson Plan 6 41

Works Cited 42

Wissenschaftlicher Buchverlag bietet
kostenfreie
Publikation
von
wissenschaftlichen Arbeiten

Diplomarbeiten, Magisterarbeiten, Master und Bachelor Theses
sowie Dissertationen, Habilitationen und wissenschaftliche Monographien

Sie verfügen über eine wissenschaftliche Abschlußarbeit zu aktuellen oder zeitlosen Fragestellungen, die hohen inhaltlichen und formalen Ansprüchen genügt, und haben **Interesse an einer honorarvergüteten Publikation**?

Dann senden Sie bitte erste Informationen über Ihre Arbeit per Email an info@vdm-verlag.de. Unser Außenlektorat meldet sich umgehend bei Ihnen.

VDM Verlag Dr. Müller Aktiengesellschaft & Co. KG
Dudweiler Landstraße 125a
D - 66123 Saarbrücken

www.vdm-verlag.de

Made in the USA